DARKNESS AND DECADENCE
The Grumblings of a Gargoyle

by Lynn Gerrard

To Jean & Joe
Best Wishes
Lynn Gerrard
AKA
The Grumbling
Gargoyle x.

Table of Contents

Published in 2015 by Wallace Publishing

Acknowledgment

Countless thanks goes to Leesa, of Wallace Publishing, for plucking my musings from the virtual and delivering them into the physical and a huge thank you goes to the wonderful Kensington Gore for recommending my work in the first place.

An immeasurable debt of gratitude is owed to my family for putting up with the constant whoosh of my mood swing: husband Michael, Mum, Bill, my much loved children Lisa, Emma, Daniel, Jade and my equally much loved grandchildren Charlie, Amber, Chloe and Isobel...who have in turn encouraged me, inspired me and ultimately reassured me...that it's ok to be weird.

And to my friends on Twitter and Facebook, Carol, Kate, Christine, Hap, Jonathon, Peter, Sharon...and so many, many more, I am forever grateful for your unrelenting support and encouragement...thank you.

Finally, thanks go to my dog Ralph, my constant companion, for staying by my side during all of my writing tantrums...and managing to sleep through most of them...I love you too.

Lynn Gerrard

Dedication:

For Uncle Tom

MELANCHOLY GARGOYLE

Melancholy Gargoyle

Dry your eyes and fly

Into the soft

And soothing embrace

Of an understanding sky

HOW QUIET THE GRAVE

How quiet the grave

To all above

Oblivious to

The noise below

As flesh begins

To decompose, liquefy

And softly slide

Away from bone

To spill upon earth

Where creatures wait

To do their worst

And feast upon the residue

Of the slimy sludge

That once was you!

A MONSTER'S LULLABY

Hush child
Shush child
Don't make a fuss child
I'll guard all your dreams whilst you sleep.

Quiet child
Rest child
The rhythm of my breath child
Will guide you to slumber's so deep

That child
Then child
Beneath the sly moon child
I'll feed on your soul
As you weep.

So hush child
Shush child
Don't make a fuss child
You're mine now forever to keep.

A TIRED BROW

Death is not a

Cowled, gnarled shape

Hungering

For your soul

Death is

The tender touch

Upon a tired brow

Come to take your

Spirit home

DEATH BED

Upon her Death Bed she did lie
And through a weak and fading croak,
Placed a wrinkled hand, upon his arm
Then squeezing lightly, spoke

'Remember what I taught you child,
Show passion in all you do,
Always put your own needs first
No one else will think of you'

He smiled and placed a loving kiss
Upon her paling cheek,
Promising he would be strong
Like her, he despised the weak.

Then stroking her grey and tired hair,
He fixed it into place
Before fluffing her pillow one last time
And pressing it over her face...

THE LOVERS

Her name was Alice and she worked in Asda
She'd just been promoted from Pet Foods to Pastas
She fancied getting married and she hoped maybe he'd ask her
One day.

His name was Martin and he was on probation
For going into PC World and nicking a Play Station
He quite fancied an ASBO and a 'Gangsta' reputation
What a prat.

Today she was excited, after work he'd said he'd meet her
So at break she'd had a spray tan and for lunch, pie with Ryvita
She'd superglued her nails on and her hair would look much neater
Later on.

He'd had a tattoo done, his third attempt at trying
To get through the procedure without persistent crying
His Mum had to collect him 'cos he'd told her he was dying
Such a nob.

So Alice, shift now over, all blinged up to meet her date
Was suddenly heartbroken and instantly irate
To see Martin chatting up Chantelle who worked on 'Freshly Baked'
What to do?

Then Martin noticed Alice and his life became much scarier

When she walked up and drop kicked him right up his thick
posterior
He landed to the words "Unwanted Item In Bagging Area"
Nuff Said!

So the moral of the story is
Martin, don't try to be notorious
When all you're really doing is
Absolutely boring us...

You pathetic little Wimp!

AN APPOINTMENT WITH DEATH

I was sat in the doctor's waiting room
Trying to catch my breath,
When an icy blast blew past me
And there, in the doorway, stood Death!

His black cloak was flapping around him,
A skeletal hand grasped his scythe,
His red eyes were burning
My stomach was churning
I couldn't have moved if I'd tried!

The noise of the silence was deafening
Not one cough or sneeze came to pass
Between the horrified onlookers,
Each staring, mouths open, gob smacked!

Death's lengthy shape remained upright
His hooded skull turned as it scanned
The quivering cowards before him
All hoping the other was damned.

Then suddenly a voice from reception
Said, "Ah Mr Reaper you're here,
Your anti-depressants are ready
And there's good news, your X - Rays are clear"

Death glided casually over
Then prescription tucked inside his cloak
His cowled form studied those waiting

And with a tone of foreboding he spoke.

"It's the fault of you self - serving mortals
That I've been depressed and so glum
But as soon as I'm better
I'm coming to get you
Oh yes friends
Won't that be fun?"

BEHIND CLOSED DOORS

Our world exists
Behind closed doors
Where we hide from being judged
By the duplicity
Of yours
Yet even here we are not safe
From the preconceptions
And the prejudice.
You see, the world out there
Needs to get to know
The people whose lives
Are lived and lost
Behind closed doors
Instead of branding and labelling
All it perceives
To be a virulent strain
Of humanity
A mental illness is not a disease
It cannot be caught
Through a cough or a sneeze
Ignorance is the germ to avoid
A contagious bug
That must be destroyed
By injecting understanding
And paving the way
Towards saving us from stigma
By stripping us of shame.

THE KID

Stick another pie in the fat kid
'Cos it's easier for you,
And sod exercise
Just feed it fries
As it's squashed into a seat for two.

Bang another game in its X Box
So you don't have to cope
With the boring themes
Of its hopes and dreams
As they're puffed away in your smoke.

Slap all the blame for your lifestyle
On the kid as it tries to sleep
To escape the pain
Slicing through its brain
Of the bullying that makes it weep.

Take another hit from your crack pipe
And let the kid sort out the mess
In the stinking hole
Of the dump that's home
Where it becomes more depressed.

Throw another punch when the money's spent
To remind the kid it's a drain
To buy it stuff
When there's hardly enough
Cash for your cocaine.

Knock another nail in its coffin
Pretend you don't know why

A kid so sweet would admit defeat
And lonely and lost
Choose to die.

OLD SOUL

The old soul peered
Through the newborn's eyes
Saddened to see
A world it recognised

Where famine and war
And disease still raged
Where compassion and peace
Remained to be upstaged

By material gain
And industrial greed
By one man challenging
Another man's creed

And the old soul sighed
Feeling pity for the child
As it drew its first breath
Before letting out a cry

FIREFLIES

Words rage around my head
Like angry fireflies
Vying for the attention
Of the flame
Desperate to be acknowledged
As burning brighter
Than any other
To earn
Prime position
On the page.
So many books
Poems
Plays
To write
And lay bare
Before the universe
Before life's ink
Runs dry
And the very words whose company
Has seen fit both to
Fuel my madness
And to appease it
Shrivel
And are cast
Into the deafened catacombs of eternity
To join the plaintive cries
Of children never to be born

A DRAGON AND A GARGOYLE

A Dragon walked with me today
We shared our thoughts along the way
Which spoke of times when kids
Would read together.

When through their books the likes of us,
A Dragon and a Gargoyle, would
Join other creatures
In all sorts of weather

To play the part of monsters vile
Devouring children with a smile
And scaring villagers
With our monstrous ways

Causing havoc where we walked
Fuelling fear when e'r we talked
Oh yes indeed
Those were happy days

But now our world is fading fast
And we're not sure how long we'll last
If children choose
To leave their books behind

In favour of a wordless world
Where lights and sounds replace the swirl
Of characters wrestling
Through the pages of the mind

So on we walk, the Dragon and I
Convinced that soon our kind will die
Should no one save the chapters
Of our lives

Already with each step we take
Our presence starts to dissipate
And now it's we
Who tremble with raw fear

No time to waste, child, grab that book
Read life back into the likes of us
There's Unicorns to ride
And Giants to slay

It's time for you to take a stand
And fight for us and this our land
A monster's hero born to us
This day

THE PATH OF YESTERDAY

To walk the path
Of yesterday
To tap upon the door
That leads to those
We've loved and lost
And be with them
Once more

GOING HOME

She can't remember who she is
Or who she used to be
She watches people come and go
Quick visits
Cups of tea

But who they are or what they want
She hasn't got a clue
She only knows that when they leave
The others will walk through

Insisting that it's time for bed
Whilst feeding her the pills
That make her head feel fuzzy
That persuade her to keep still

And through the night her frail old form
Will cry out for release
Yet no one will come tend to her
To put her mind at ease.

Then come the morning at first light
Her cries, ignored as yet,
Will turn to doleful whimpers
As she shivers in the wet

Until at last the others come
And seeing all her mess
Roughly drag her ancient bones
And curse whilst they undress

The sobbing woman filled with shame
For all that she's become
As lucid moments beg to ask
Just what it is she has done

To deserve the kind of treatment
That she suffers every day
And so she prays for Jesus
To carry her away

To where her love is waiting
And with arms outstretched will he
Hold her closely once again
And restore her dignity.

HEART ATTACK

Hear the pitter patter
Of the fatted dripping batter
As your heart begins to chatter
In your chest.

Feel your body stumble
As your senses start to crumble
Until through a groaning tumble
You're at rest

HUMANITY

I nailed his heart
To a Rainbow
And watched the colours
Bleed.

I chained his Soul
To an Angel
To infect her with his
Seed.

I fed his pain
To an innocent
To enjoy her tortured
Pleas.

I poured his misery
On humanity
That I may bathe in its disease

CLOSURE

He held her tiny hand in his,
Whilst through a choked
And trembling voice
Apologised for all he'd done
Said he didn't have a choice
The beast inside controlled him
Made him do the things he did
Then placing the tape across her mouth
He closed the coffin lid.

MANKIND

Drenched in the tears of Angels
Unaffected by their celestial despair
Mankind marches forward
With determined tread
Crushing beneath him
The soulless carcasses
Whose worthless shapes
Form the festering Road to Hell.

LIFE

You preach about the sanctity of life
Through teeth littered with the remnants of my flesh.
Surrounded by your brethren you wallow in the smugness of
your choices
Yet allow me none.

Together you decry the horror of those captive to their hunger
As you and yours devour all before you.
Oh pulpiteer of precious sentience
Am I deserving of this ignorance?

You wouldn't know.
Consider! Dear Vegetarian, so conscious of the pulse,
That I the humble Lettuce...Also have a heart.

NO SALADS FOR SONIA

No salads for Sonya
You can stick 'em up your arse
Just pass the cream buns
And daily dose of forty fags

No gym whims for Sonya
Sod that rubbish, why should she
Let the ties of exercise
Prise her from the settee!

No lemonade for Sonya
She likes her vodka neat
In vast amounts, who's keeping count!
She's no mind to be discreet

No lectures for Sonya
She doesn't need your spiel
Of conscience nudging, lifestyle judging
Crap to spoil her meal!

No energy for Sonya
She's not feeling too good
Even fries and a couple of pies
Aren't pleasing her as they should

No visitors for Sonya
The nurse says that won't do
Her any good, not that it could
Whilst she's wired up in ICU

No tears for Sonya

Just shaking heads and talking
Of had she listened, her present position
Wouldn't be her in a coffin!

THE CHANGE

We've changed and shifted
Moved and drifted
Things are not
As they were

He's almost indifferent
To my very existence
He sees through me
As if I'm not there

In bed he lies huddled
Denying me cuddles
Should I dare to brush
Past his flesh

I speak and he quivers
He cowers and shivers
He's just not the same man
Since my death

NIGHT ON THE PROWL

Middle aged women
With their young-girl shoes
In their scary short skirts
Bellies bulging full of booze

Prowling the night clubs
Hunting for a fella
Far too pissed to notice
He's about to pull Godzilla

False eyelashes flapping
'Maybe It's Maybelline'
Onlookers thinking
'Maybe it's just obscene'

Thick foundation cracking
Pushing out a smile
Through a predatory maw
Last seen on a crocodile

A handbag holding fags
And lipstick, shades of crazy,
Nuzzled 'tween spare knickers
Hiding packs of 'Tena Lady'

With a head full of hope
And a heart full of hurt
They totter on their tarty way
Whilst hoisting up their skirts.

OVER THE EDGE

The body hung from the banister
With all the grace of a butchered carcass in an abattoir.
She wasn't sure how long she'd been staring at it
From her prime position on the stairs
But its spreading putrescence suggested it had been some
time.
She didn't care.

She was far too happy to consider such trivia.
Far too relieved at the prospect of finally being set free
From the vicious cruelty that had crippled her life for so long.
A delighted yet hushed observer
Throughout the entertaining process of the body's demise,
She wanted to extend her joy in every nuance of its agonies.
It was only right.

Smiling, her eyes slowly glided down the taut pull
Of the bright blue plastic washing line and decided
It had never been put to better use.
Such a strong line too for one so inexpensive,
Firmly holding and maintaining the weight
Of the jerking, dancing figure, with some ease
As it had thrashed out its final insults
And so able to sustain the corruption of such strain
During the beauty of its present state.
Impressive.

Bulging, sightless eyes hypnotised her with the menace of
their viscous gaze,
Reminiscent of the constant torture she had suffered
For so many years under their mocking scrutiny.
But that was of the past now

And she laughed as she watched globules of mucous
Erupt from their foul haven
Before oozing their gloop over bloated, benumbed cheeks.
Tears of remorse at last?
How fitting, she smirked.

She marvelled with much interest
As two purple, swollen lips nursed a tongue
So thickened by the virility of deaths surge
As to finally render it incapable of the vile miseries
It had once so loudly and relentlessly inflicted
Upon the innocent senses of others.
Still, despite the merriment of this splendidly putrid theatre
She gained most pleasure from the stilled offences
Of those dreadful fingers.

Never again would they point and poke and slash and stab at
her fragility.
No more would they mark her worthlessness
With thunderous applause before tearing at her hair
And pushing her beyond the brink of sanity.
Her head was clear now.
Her mind at rest.
She had done what was right.

She had saved herself and others from endless persecution.
Her euphoria was interrupted by one final consideration,
That if she hadn't been such a bitch in life
Maybe her troubled spirit wouldn't be left here
Staring at the slow decomposition
Of her own rotting corpse.

PANIC ATTACK

I'm frightened to drift
To slip
To slide
Will you stop me?

I'm beginning to tremble
To shake
To shiver
Will you hold me?

I'm starting to gasp
To choke
To die
Will you save me?

I'm going to flip
To fall
To drop
Will you catch me?

I'm needing to flee
To run
To hide
Will you find me?

I'm wanting to stop
To start
To live
Will you help me?
Help set me free...

THE BOX

Just a girl and already a Mother
Three kids at her heels and expecting another
With her face worn and worried it was hard to dispel
The irony of her T Shirt which boldly claimed 'Rebel'.

She'd married young to escape stuff at home
An only child who they wouldn't leave alone
All their shouting and fighting and booze fuelled screams
Would deny her the safety and sanctuary of dreams.

So she ran into the arms of her very own Prince Charming
Convinced their love was real and whilst his manner was
alarming
He'd only hit her once or twice and had told her he was sorry
Said the alcohol had blurred his vision, turning lover into
quarry.

Then the babies came quite rapidly and everything got worse
If his hands weren't reaching for her throat they were
grabbing for her purse
So she took her Hurt and Heartbreak and she put them in a
box
And lay them next to Love and Hope and then she turned the
lock.

She'd deal with feelings one fine day but now amidst the
storm
Her only care was for the kids and keeping them from harm
She'd take them and she'd find a place where they'd all be set
free
And bury the box of feelings and hide away the key.

Who knows, perhaps the day would come where she could trust again
But for now she'd build her children's dreams, there was no room for men
She'd swim against the tide once more, she'd never let them drown
Life might throw stuff at her
But it would never drag her down

REMOVAL

I have no idea what time the truck arrived
It was just there,
Outside the house,
Uncovered,
Dirty,
Emotionless.

One by one her treasures were piled into it
Without thought,
Or care.
Quickly,
Impatiently,
Recklessly.

Laden, the removal men chatted as they passed the other
Fags dangling from lips,
Sharing a joke,
Laughing,
Disrespectful,
Mocking.

And all the while, her life's story continued to lie naked
Before the elements,
On public display,
Exposed,
Vulnerable,
Mournful.

Each item thrown with disregard into the truck still bore the shadows
Of so many hopes and dreams
Long past,

Irretrievable now,
Fading,
Forgotten.

Forever silenced by Death, no more would these remnants of
life
Stand to tell her tale
Of love,
Passion,
Pleasure,
Pain.

Nor could I.
Whoever she had been in life I do not know
I was just a passer - by,
An observer,
A stranger,
Of no consequence.
And still I cried
For the loss of her.

THERE WAS A TIME

There was a time, my friend,
There was a time,
But now those times have gone,
And the dreams we used to dream back then
Are now just Once Upon.
Like grains of sand through fingers
Measured moments swiftly sift
Blowing through our yesterdays
As we finally start to drift
Away from all we used to be
To the place where we now stand
Holding the others memories,
No longer holding the others hand.

OH FOR THOSE DAYS

I stepped inside
An old photograph
And sat with you a while
Your eyes though shocked
To see me
Couldn't hide the smile
That flitted 'cross
The rosy lips
That I knew so well
The very same
Whose teasing games
Had cast me under their spell

Oh for those days again
My love
When youths flush held us firm
When time was everlasting
For that young boy and his girl
Oh for those days once more
My love
And every night I pray
When next I step into
Your photograph
I'll finally get to stay

THE BROKEN HEART

I saw a broken heart today
And although it wasn't mine
As every fretful fragment fell
Inside, my own heart cried
To watch the other's agony
To see their world implode
Destroyed by yet another heart
But let's not judge too soon
The other heart was hurting too
For the loss of that which was
And the that which was
Was full of love but
Feelings have moved on
And so Goodbye it has to be
As all hearts did concede
The only way true love is found
Is when it is set free

THE COUNSELLOR

She sorts my head
And soothes my mind
She helps me cope
When dark thoughts blind
My pain she sees
Yet is unaware
I also see
The pain in her

THE DARK

Within my Septic Palace
Tortured souls adorn the walls
Whereupon their screams are smothered
By the creatures that there crawl

As they slide their slithering tendrils
Through putrid peals of glee
Around the jellied, quivering shapes
Bound in bile for eternity.

Yet there is a greater misery
And it threatens my gangrenous lair
'Tis a horror of such noxious nast
As to give this Demon a scare

With the boldness and the brightness
Of all the light it brings
As it unburdens membranous mucous
From that whorish womb called
Spring

SILKEN DREAMS

He comes to me in silken dreams
Where, with gentle haste,
Velvet threads of comfort are cast
Upon my furrowed brow,
Dulling the barbed edges
Of my cruel melancholies.

He speaks not to me
And yet, through the shimmering
Vapours of his presence,
Which rest with quiet grace upon my soul,
I know all of him and am calmed.

Tender melodies shaped by unfamiliar chords
Enfold me within their phantom embrace
Serving to rest me upon a cloud
Of such harmonies as would provide
Eternal succour from the mischief of life's plagues

Harm will not find me here,
Solace is my companion, Sanctuary my saviour
I belong here, with him.
We are one.
And knowing this...

At last I am at peace

And sleep on.

THE WINDOW

Looking wistfully through
The window of my past
With a knowing finger
I softly dare to tap
Upon the glass
Where yesterday still holds
A chance for me to live
My life's lost goals

FILTH

Our Affair is not for the flowery words of poets
Or the courteous colours upon an artist's canvas,
Our affair is for the dark, dirty, raw, unfettered filth
That lurks within the tapestry of our
Mindful dwellings.

I hold no shame for my thoughts, my longings,
My want, my need to hold your majesty within my opened
palm
And marvel at its fleeing flaccidity
As the current of life's juice engorges this vibrant vessel
With its urgency to be tended...and to tend.

I feel only the thrill of enclosing my eager fingers
Around such glorious girth,
Trembling in anticipation
Of what is to come.

With your vulnerability held firmly in my hand
I control you.
I am your Mistress.
You will obey me.

You are mine to take and do with as I so choose.
You will not speak.
You will not utter one sound
Other than the moans and groans
Of approaching ecstasies as I push and pull and guide
Your vulgar rigidity,
Without care or compassion,
Into every foul crevice of my liking.

As I sense the strain of your impending surge begging for release
I will hold a while
Until your heat subsides and then I will upon you once again.
Harder this time,
Driving you further into the murky depths of my sinful sanctuary,
Pounding and thrusting with forceful intent
To finish the job in hand.

Then at last I empty you
And we are spent.
My gluttony appeased for the moment,
You are dismissed until the next time
My insatiable hunger seeks your ever pleasing services
And then I shall once again...Delve into the Debauched Delight
That is you...
My Dyson Vacuum Cleaner!

THE SPELL

Of Raven's Beak
Of Vulture's Breath
Of all things Dark
That walk with Death
Of Shapes that Twist
And things that Bite
The Spell is Spoke
I Own the Night

THE ME WE ARE

How can we ever
'Find ourselves'
When every day
We're someone else?
"What do you mean by that"?
I hear you ask.

Well, every person
And every deed
That touches your life,
You must concede,
Folds and moulds and shapes
Just where we're at!

The me I am when I'm with you
Is not the me I am with someone new
But bits of you, through me,
Are passed to them

Then they, in turn, pass on their stuff
To others they meet
And sure enough
Together the me we are is carried through!

So enjoy the person
You are today
Who knows who, tomorrow
Will come your way
Transforming, once again your personal form

And call off the search to find yourself
'Cos most of you is someone else
Just hope that you and they can get along!

THE END?

Gone
Without my knowing.
Leaving in your wake a few ragged shreds,
Mere fragments of the time we used to share.

Sitting here, alone, devoid of your essential presence
My mind burrows into its cavernous depths
Searching for a means of understanding.

Why did those closest to me
Choose to smother the knowledge of your impending exit?
Had they but uttered one single word
There could have been change perhaps
Enough to save us from this bottomless misery.

Oh how I miss your velvet touch upon my cheek
The quilted warmth of your embrace however fleeting.
Still, until such time as another takes your place
I shall remain seated here
Constantly wondering
Why am I the only one to change the bloody toilet roll?